Communicate with Quality

COMMUNICATE WITH QUALITY:

Tips and Techniques for Continuous Improvement of the Communications Process

Dr. Marlene Caroselli

PUBLISHED BY
Center for Professional Development
10305 Summertime Lane
Culver City, California 90230

Copyright © 1990 by Marlene Caroselli
All rights reserved. No part of the contents of this book may be reproduced or transmitted in any form or by any means without the written permission of the publisher.

ISBN 0-922411-01-8

Printed and bound in the United States of America. Second printing: June 1991

TABLE OF CONTENTS

Introduction.. page 3

Chapter 1: The Composing Process............................ page 5
    Five Techniques for Getting Started   page 5
    Four Patterns of Organization   page 11
Ameliorating Your Affect..*page* 17

Chapter 2: The Editing Process: Vocabulary and Spelling........ page 18
    100 Commonly Confused Words   page 18
    Tone   page 24
    10 Alternatives to Hackneyed Conclusions   page 24
    10 Additional Tone Problems   page 25
    10 Ways to Avoid Sexist Language   page 29
    50 Most Frequently Misspelled Words   page 32
    15 Spelling Rules   page 35
    13 Rules for Using Hyphens   page 38
Ameliorating Your Affect..*page* 40

Chapter 3: The Editing Process: Grammar............................ page 41
    16 Marks of Punctuation   page 41
    Diagnostic Test   page 44
    10 Capitalization Rules   page 46
    Diagnostic Tests   page 48
    Syntax Concepts   page 51
    Diagnostic Test   page 52
Ameliorating Your Affect..*page* 57

Chapter 4: The Proofreading Process.................................. page 58
    12 Proofreading Techniques   page 58
    Practice Exercises   page 61
    Formats/Format Consistency   page 71
    Proofreading Symbols   page 76
    Checklist   page 79
Ameliorating Your Affect..*page* 80

Chapter 5: Telephone Techniques...................................... page 81
    30 Things to Avoid When on the Phone   page 85
    40 Tips for Projecting Professionalism   page 87
    Additional Ameliorating-Your-Affect Exercises............*page* 97

Answer Key   page 100

INTRODUCTION

Achieving excellence in written expression is a three-step process:

1. The composing stage
2. The editing stage
3. The proofreading stage.

In this workbook, we shall examine some proven practices for helping you to compose more quickly, to edit more precisely, to proofread more carefully. In addition, we shall explore techniques for helping you project a more professional image when communicating by telephone.

As you know by now, you are judged by the way you use words. Think for a moment about how much emphasis our society places on the proper use of words. One obvious example is the fact that high school students have their potential for handling college-level work judged on two accounts: the verbal and the mathematical.

When you hear someone speak like this -- "I...ah..you know, I...ain't gonna...never do dat...you know...again." -- you probably assume immediately the person is not very intelligent. In fact, intelligence is a relative thing, and the speaker who fumbles verbally may be intelligent in his own way. Many academicians (J. P. Guilford, for example) believe there are many more indices of intelligence than one's ability to manipulate words or numbers.

But the truth remains that our intelligence is assessed whenever we speak our ideas or put them on paper. This inevitable assessment is enough to paralyze some writers, making them hate the writing process, postpone it as often as they can, and -- when they can avoid it no longer -- go through a lengthy and torturous process of getting their thoughts down on paper. Other people have a similar response when the stimulus is the need to address a group.

It need not be like that!

If you can grow to regard writing or speaking as an adventure, a way of sharing your thoughts clearly and concisely, you will find a new confidence emerging. That confidence will be born of knowing that others -- when they read or hear your excellent expression of thoughts -- will judge you an articulate, intelligent person, in full command of language.

So, if you have been used to fulminating about the communication process:

> "I never learned to diagram sentences."
> "English was always my worst subject."
> "I just can't seem to get my thoughts on paper."
> "All my English teachers hated me."
> "I have to rewrite everything at least two times."
> "Mrs. Hogeboom in tenth grade made fun of my dangling participles and I've hated English ever since."
> "I'm afraid I'm going to use the wrong word."
> "I'm just not a good speller."
> "I can't write under pressure."
> "I can't talk into a telephone message machine."
> "That darn phone is always interrupting me."

put these negative feelings behind you and prepare to embark upon an adventure which -- if it doesn't make you enjoy the communicating process -- will at least make you more proficient at it.

Think of how your productivity will increase when you have succeeded in reducing your composing-editing-proofreading time. And consider the pride you will feel in knowing that you are handling the telephone not as an enemy but as another aspect of your job in which you can demonstrate mastery. The proven practices in this workbook will enable you to improve both your writing and your speaking skills.

Organizations in which you work should not just be viewed as "the employer." Organizations are contexts in which you can learn and grow; they are groups of experienced people who are willing to pass their knowledge on to you, to demonstrate their skills so you can improve yours, and to give you an opportunity to try your wings in an environment that no one person could create.

--Margaret Higginson and Thomas Quick

Chapter 1: The Composing Process

Five Techniques for Getting Started

The sight of a blank page creates instant mental anguish for many business writers. Yet, that blank page <u>can</u> be viewed as an invitation, a challenge to create a written communication that will share meaning, or solve a problem, or persuade colleagues to undertake a new idea. Here are five techniques for helping you to convey your ideas from your head to that blank sheet quickly and painlessly.

1. Scribble Sheet

Albert Einstein estimated he was only using 25% of his mental capacity. The rest of us, scientists estimate, are only employing 1-10% of our brain power. Your mind has an amazing capacity for generating ideas -- all you have to do is tap into that power.

The scribble-sheet technique allows you to quickly record those ideas exploding inside your head and then refine those ideas by integrating them into a cohesive composition.

In the center of that blank sheet of paper, write down the key word or words around which your next letter or memo should focus. Then quickly -- without stopping to censure your ideas or to worry about spelling --

Communicate with Quality

jot down all the related ideas that spring into your mind. Just write words, not whole sentences. You will soon have a scribble sheet filled with information to be included in your communication.

Now, go back to that scribble sheet and begin to organize the information: draw arrows among the ideas which naturally go together. Cross out those which do not fit. Group the ideas under large headings. The whole process will not take more than five minutes and will supply you with all the facts or points you need.

Let's try it. Here is the topic:

Your boss has asked you to prepare a brief memo reminding employees about the Adopt-a-School Program and your organization's interest in it. He is especially anxious to have employees volunteer to talk to students about entry-level qualifications. Use this page to organize your thoughts for this memo.

Any writer overwhelmingly honest about pleasing himself is almost sure to please others.
— Marianne Moore

2. Free Association

The second technique is like "stream-of-consciousness" writing, in that you will begin writing whatever is in your mind about the given topic. At times, your mind will wander into unrelated areas, but keep on writing. Soon enough, your brain will re-direct itself to the subject you should be concentrating on. The brain is never at a loss for words; it never stops thinking. So just record those thoughts in your mind -- as quickly as you can -- for a five-to-ten minute period.

Topic: Your boss has asked you to write a brief essay on an upcoming holiday. She would like to publish your thoughts in the next issue of the company newsletter. Use this space to freely associate your thoughts.

With sixty staring me in the face, I have developed a definite hardening of the paragraphs.
                                             --James Thurber at age 59

3. The F-A-S-T Technique

In the business world, we do not always have the luxury of writing at our leisure. Sometimes, we are under pressure to get a written communication out to others in a limited time span. The F-A-S-T technique will help you compose letters, memos and even impromptu speeches when you do not have hours to devote to the topic.

Here's how it works:

- F = Focus/ State the focus or main idea of the communication.
- A = Amplify/ Amplify or expand upon the focus, perhaps by giving background material.
- S = Specify/ State the specifics or give examples.
- T = Tie/ Tie it all up; summarize; offer a recommendation.

<u>Topic</u>: You need to send a memo to co-workers reminding them of what you would like to have them do during your absence. Begin by stating the focus of your memo, amplify that focus, give specifics and then tie it up. Use the space below.

Focus:

Amplify:

Specify:

Tie:

Words ought to be a little wild, for they are the assault of thought on the unthinking.
--John Maynard Keynes

4. The P-I-E Approach

This approach will keep you on target in your writing, for it forces you to supply answers to three specific questions:

- P = Purpose/ What is the purpose for this memo?
- I = Information/ What information does the reader need?
- E = End result/ What do I want the reader to do as a result of having read this communication?

Apply the P-I-E technique to the following topic:

Your boss has asked you to informally survey the members of your department to see if they would be interested in having a lunch-time seminar program. You have found there is considerable interest among your colleagues. Write a memo to your boss to launch the program.

Purpose:

Information Needed:

End Result:

Make every word tell. --Strunk and White

5. Sectioning

Another approach which will aid in organizing your thoughts rapidly is the Sectioning approach. When you have only a general idea of the topic of your communication, Sectioning will help you break down that broad topic into particular categories. Use a heading for each section and then fill in related ideas under those headings. For example, if you were to write about technology of the future, your section headlines might be computers/ space/medicine/transportation/robotics.

<u>Topic</u>: Jot down the broad classifications for a memo you have to write concerning the office Christmas party, which you have been asked to organize. Beneath each section heading, write related ideas. Use this space.

When in doubt, strike it out. —Mark Twain

Four Patterns of Organization

For longer documents, you should have a specific pattern of organization around which the data can be assembled. When you are drafting documents, it will help you to write the selected pattern in big letters at the top of the page. That way, you will be reminded to include only relevant material.

1. Problem-Solution

Much business writing uses the Problem-Solution pattern. This method forces the writer to state clearly and simply the nature of the problem under discussion. Then, in the second half of the communication, the writer merely states the solution being offered for the problem. Develop the topic below into a well-constructed memo using two simple focal points: the problem and its solution.

<u>Topic:</u> Who makes the coffee in the morning has become an issue among the members of your department. In the past, the secretary always assumed that responsibility (which also entailed keeping the coffee area clean). You feel it more equitable to have the coffee responsibilities handled on a monthly basis by different members of the department. Write a memo discussing the problem and offering your solution.

2. Sequence

The Sequence Pattern forces you to think in a linear fashion: you progress logically from one idea to the next. Order is critical in the Sequence Pattern; your reader will become confused if you lack exactness or clarity in ordering events. A sequential progression is especially important in writing instructions.

Topic: Think about the position you hope to hold five or ten years from today. Then write an action plan to yourself and for yourself, describing the sequential steps you must take in order to achieve this desired position. If you plan to be doing in five or ten years exactly what you are doing today, then shift your topic to your plans for retirement and write an action plan for that eventuality.

My pencils outlast their erasures. --Vladimir Nabokov

3. General-to-Specific/Specific-to-General

Depending on the psychological effect you wish to convey, you can use either the General-to-Specific or the Specific-to-General Pattern to persuade the reader that your point-of-view is a convincing one.

If your intent is to make a bold opening statement and then proceed to win over your reader by providing specific supporting details, you will use the General-to-Specific approach.

On the other hand, if you feel your reader would respond better to a careful, deliberate buildup of your argument -- with your request or viewpoint stated last -- you should use the Specific-to-General pattern.

Topic: Discuss the nature of your company and its product or services, using either of the two approaches described above.

The writer must teach himself that the basest of all things is to be afraid.
--William Faulkner

4. Rational

The key word to be considered when using the Rational Pattern of Organization is the word "because." With this pattern, you will be supplying your rationale: the reason(s) why you have decided to embark upon a particular course of action.

Topic: You would like to attend a specific training program which would mean being away from your job for one full week next month. You, of course, would prefer not to use your vacation time for this week-long educational pursuit. Write a memo to your boss, attempting to persuade her of your rationale. Supply several reasons why you believe you should be given this time off with pay to attend this seminar.

Exercise in Giving Instructions

As you participate in this exercise, make notes here about the effectiveness of the instructions given. Can you extend your observations from this microcosmic activity to the macrocosmic business world?

Communicating in the Corporate Realm

1. Especially when giving directions, plan in advance what you will say or write.

2. Give an overview of what the ultimate product or outcome is expected to be. Provide the skeleton to which subsequent "flesh" will be added.

3. Assure your audience that they can reach success.

4. Encourage questions; they help clarify the task. Listen carefully to others.

5. Recognize that words are subject to multiple interpretations.

6. Employ kinesics or body language whenever you can; study the body language of others.

7. Repeat key points and monitor the work in progress to ensure participants understand their task.

8. Challenge (or at least define) the constraints you believe confine you.

9. Make no assumptions.

10. Use visual aids.

11. Stop at appropriate intervals to review what should have been done up to this point. Obtain feedback about what is really happening.

12. Present a summary.

Ameliorating Your Affect toward Lexical Acquisition

The skilled writer is able to use the appropriate words at the appropriate time. While a rich vocabulary has been shown repeatedly to correlate with success in business, there is a danger in using words that a given reader might not understand.

For example, you actually know the meaning of these sentences. But -- because the vocabulary is so difficult -- it is hard to figure out what the sentences are really saying. How many of these sesquipedalian structures can you figure out?

1. Scintillate, scintillate, asteroid minific.

2. Neophyte's serendipity.

3. It is futile to endeavor to indoctrinate a superannuated canine with innovations.

4. Pulchritude possesses solely cutaneous profundity.

5. The stylus is more potent than the claymore.

6. Surveillance should precede saltation.

7. Members of an avian species possessing similar plumage tend to be gregarious.

8. It is futile to engage in lacrimation concerning precipitively removed lacteal fluid.

9. Freedom from incrustations of grime is contiguous to divinity.

10. Eschew the implement of correction and vitiate the scion.

Communicate with Quality

Chapter 2: The Editing Process

Vocabulary

100 Commonly Confused Words

While there is no denying the importance of an extensive vocabulary, sometimes it is the little words, the familiar, everyday words, that cause damage to our reputations as language masters. Here are 100 frequently confused and misused words. Write a short sentence for each; try to show the meaning of the word by its use in the sentence. If you are not certain of the meaning of certain words, look them up in the dictionary to ensure correct usage.

1. accept (verb) _____

2. except (preposition) _____

3. affect (verb) _____

4. affect (noun) _____

5. effect (verb) _____

6. effect (noun) _____

7. activate (verb) _____

8. actuate (verb) _____

9. adapt (verb) _____

Communicate with Quality

10 adept (adjective) _____

11 adopt (verb) _____

12 adverse (adjective) _____

13 averse (adjective) _____

14 allude (verb) _____

15 elude (verb) _____

16 alumnus (noun) _____

17 alumna (noun) _____

18 apprehend (verb) _____

19 comprehend (verb) _____

20 assay (verb) _____

21 essay (verb) _____

22 avocation (noun) _____

23 vocation (noun) _____

24 bisect (verb) _____

25 dissect (verb) _____

26 carat (noun) _____

27 caret (noun) _____

28 carrot (noun) _____

29 casual (adjective) _____

Communicate with Quality

30 causal (adjective) _____

31 catholic (adjective) _____

32 Catholic (adjective) _____

33 compose (verb) _____

34 comprise (verb) _____

35 comprehensible (adjective) _____

36 comprehensive (adjective) _____

37 concave (adjective) _____

38 convex (adjective) _____

39 confidant (noun) _____

40 confident (adjective) _____

41 connotation (noun) _____

42 denotation (noun) _____

43 consensus (noun) _____

44 corespondent (noun) _____

45 correspondent (noun) _____

46 decisive (adjective) _____

47 incisive (adjective) _____

48 defective (adjective) _____

49 deficient (adjective) _____

Communicate with Quality

50 definite (adjective) _____

51 definitive (adjective) _____

52 deprecate (verb) _____

53 depreciate (verb) _____

54 discomfort (noun) _____

55 discomfit (verb) _____

56 discomfiture (noun) _____

57 discreet (adjective) _____

58 discrete (adjective) _____

59 disinterested (adjective) _____

60 uninterested (adjective) _____

61 disposal (noun) _____

62 disposition (noun) _____

63 dissemble (verb) _____

64 disassemble (verb) _____

65 distinctive (adjective) _____

66 distinct (adjective) _____

67 elemental (adjective) _____

68 elementary (adjective) _____

69 eleemosynary (adjective) _____

21

Communicate with Quality

70 emerge (verb) _____

71 immerge (verb)_____

72 energize (verb) _____

73 enervate (verb) _____

74 envelop (verb) _____

75 envelope (noun) _____

76 endemic (adjective) _____

77 epidemic (adjective)_____

78 epitaph (noun) _____

79 epithet (noun) _____

80 explicit (adjective) _____

81 implicit (adjective) _____

82 felicitous (adjective) _____

83 fortuitous (adjective) _____

84 flair (noun) _____

85 flare (noun) _____

86 flaunt (verb) _____

87 flout (verb) _____

88 foreword (noun) _____

89 forward (verb) _____

Communicate with Quality

90 gambit (noun) _____

91 gamut (noun) _____

92 gantlet (noun) _____

93 gauntlet (noun) _____

94 gourmand (noun) _____

95 gourmet (noun) _____

96 grateful (adjective) _____

97 gratified (adjective) _____

98 habitat (noun) _____

99 habitant (noun) _____

100 habitue (noun)_____

American English came of age long ago as a written and spoken language. Its intrinsic sounds are as beautiful and effective as any English anywhere and like a rich mother lode, it is ours for the digging.   --Dorothy Uris

TONE

The tone of our written communications should match the intent. Sometimes, a single word might convey an impression or tone contrary to what was intended. For example, the word "today" usually has a neutral connotation. But in the sentence which follows, the word "today" creates a negative impression -- quite different from the pride with which the writer was describing his firm.

> "Today, the ABC Company is dedicated to providing an excellent widget, produced by excellent employees."

The sentence implies that in the past, ABC was not at all concerned with product excellence.

10 Alternatives to Hackneyed Conclusions

In business writing, we should reflect or convey a feeling of respect, courtesy, sincerity, and firmness when necessary. Stereotypical language suggests that the writer did not care enough to express an original thought. The following sentence, for example, usually appears at the end of letters and -- because it has a hackneyed tone -- is often disregarded.

"If you have any further questions, please do not hesitate to contact me."

Here are suitable alternatives to that trite expression.

1. Know that you can call me if you have any other questions concerning this matter.

2. Should you require further details, please call.

3. If I have not provided all the information you need, please let me know.

4. Please call me if you need clarification. My number is ....

5. Here is my phone number: 555-1212. Call me if you wish to discuss this arrangement further.

Communicate with Quality

6. I am usually in my office by 8:30 a.m. Contact me then if you require additional details.

7. I hope we can discuss this matter soon. I will call within the next several days to set up a meeting.

8. I trust this letter has provided you with the necessary information. However, should you require more, just call me.

9. Feel free to contact me should you need further clarification.

10 If you feel this situation merits further attention, please contact me.

10 Additional Tone Problems

Rewrite the following sentences to improve the tone.

Example: From negative to positive:

We can't have the proposal ready until July 10.
We will have your proposal to you by July 10.

1. You will not be reimbursed for tuition unless you attend an accredited college.

_____

_____

From sarcastic to cooperative:

2. Obviously, the secretaries in your department don't realize we are operating on an austerity budget. If they did, they would never have suggested we have a company picnic to honor them on Secretary's Day.

_____

25

Communicate with Quality

_____

_____

From insulting to pleasantly firm:

3. It is difficult for me to believe that your assistant was unaware of your schedule that morning.

_____

_____

From dramatic to more balanced:

4. We were shocked to learn you will be leaving the firm.

_____

_____

From obsequious to polite:

5. I would be deeply grateful indeed if you could find time in your undeniably busy schedule to spend a few minutes with this neophyte so I could become more familiar about this terribly important subject on which you are an acknowledged expert.

_____

_____

_____

From pompous to straightforward:

6. The juxtaposition of the integral elements of this proposal with the empirical evidence from our current practices leads me to conclude that fuliginous fenestration is not an issue with which we need be concerned.

_____

_____

_____

From too-flattering to more sincere:

7. When a person of your eminent qualifications deigns to spend time with someone in a lesser position such as my own, I can only tell you that I am impressed by your dedication to excellence and your obvious concern for your employees.

_____

_____

_____

From ridiculing to simple disagreement:

8. That's the dumbest suggestion I've ever heard!

_____

_____

From long-winded to concise:

9. It is the purpose of this memorandum to advise you of the fact that, in my opinion, the implementation of the plan is essential as well as crucial

for the intended success of the operation in which we are currently engaged and for which we have displayed admirable teamwork thus far.

_____

_____

_____

From apologetic to direct:

10. It is with considerable embarrassment and deep regret that I am writing to advise of the delay in your shipment, resulting from an admittedly unforgivable act of inefficiency on our part.

_____

_____

_____

Style

Closely related to tone is the style of writing the author employs. Just as we are identified with a certain style of dress (casual, elegant, color-coordinated) or with a certain style of speech (ungrammatical, informal, peppered-with-jargon), so too can we develop a certain style of writing and alter it to fit various occasions and audiences.

We are moving slowly from a formal business writing style to a more conversational one, and from a masculine-oriented language to a less sexist one. The good business writer, whenever appropriate, will try to make her writing style an inviting one as well. (Research shows that very few executives will take the time to read a report in its entirety. It is hard to capture and hold your busy reader's attention. Why not make the style one which will whet and maintain your reader's appetite?)

Compare these two statements. Which one piques your interest and encourages you to read further into the report?

1. I have reviewed the preliminary data (as depicted in this report) and have arrived at the conclusion that we must meet again to discuss the feasibility of the proposal. Will the first week in August work for you?

2. When you learn of the cost-saving possibilities in this proposal, you will probably want to meet to discuss how to implement them. I'll keep the first week in August open for us to meet.

You probably felt the second communication was more appealing. Note that it begins with the "you" factor, whereas the first begins with the "I" factor. The second also gets directly to the word which attracts most business people: "cost-saving."

The first memo has a first-person perspective -- "I have reviewed" and "[I] have arrived at the conclusion." The suggestion to meet is less heavy-handed in the second memo: "you will probably want to meet." The choice of words is a telling factor, too: preliminary data versus cost-saving possibilities.

If you are serious about moving toward excellent expression, you will not overlook the impressions created by the tone and style of your messages!

10 Ways to Avoid Sexist Language

Sensitivity to non-offensive usage of gender-words can sometimes be carried to an extreme. For example, a secretary in a property management firm once addressed a letter to "Gentlepersons" because she felt the word "Gentlemen" was sexist.

Similarly, some people feel "shim" is an acceptable pronoun to combine the male and female references.

An ardent feminist in an audience once objected to the speaker's use of "chairman." Happy to oblige, he changed it to "chairperson." The feminist again complained -- pointing out that the word "chairperson" still ended with a masculine reference.

One of the oldest hotels in Albuquerque has written on its restaurant menu:

> "If you wish to know more about the Specialities of the House, please consult your waitperson."

Here are common-sense rules about sexist language; they have gained wide acceptance in the business world.

1. Alternate gender references, either by instance or by page.

<u>She</u> may not be willing to type and <u>he</u> may not be willing to file. Call upon your boss' expertise when the time is convenient for <u>her</u>. Each supervisor utilizes <u>his</u> staff in a different way.

2. Change references from singular to plural.

Supervisors utilize <u>their</u> staffs in different ways.

3. Use a woman's full name if you are not certain of her marital status. Or, use the abbreviation "Ms."

Dear <u>Mary Jones</u> or Dear <u>Ms</u>. Jones instead of Dear <u>Mrs</u>. Jones

4. Use the person's full name if the first name may belong to either sex.

Dear <u>Kim Jones</u> rather than Dear <u>Mr</u>. Jones

5. Never use the word "girl" or "gal" when referring to female employees.

Communicate with Quality

6. Select non-sexist words as substitutions for words which begin or end with the word "man."

businessperson instead of businessman
employee instead of workman

7. Avoid putting the word "woman" in front of a position which may have been primarily held by men in the past.

attorney instead of woman attorney
physician instead of female doctor
judge instead of lady judge

8. Change possessive pronouns to simple articles when appropriate.

The manager presented the schedule to the staff, instead of
The manager presented his schedule to his staff.

9. Use a footnote qualifier to explain that your choice of one particular gender pronoun applies to both genders equally.

*To make the writing and the reading of this document easier, the words "she" and "her" will be used to refer to managers. These pronouns are meant to apply to both genders equally, and are only employed in a single gender to avoid awkward expression.

10. Use "he/she" and "him/her" instead of single-gender references.

Each secretary is responsible for his or her own work area.

Cut! Cut! Cut! --Strunk and White

Communicate with Quality

50 Most Frequently Misspelled Words

There are those who believe they will never again have to worry about misspelled words, now that word processors with their spell-check programs are part of most office environments. But there are numerous occasions in our lives when we will not have access to word processors. Then, the ability to spell correctly will prove to be quite valuable.

On the following pages you will find a test of the 50 most frequently misspelled words in our language. Look over the two choices and select the spelling you believe is the correct one.

1. pronunciation   pronounciation
2. occasion   ocassion
3. assisstant   assistant
4. repitition   repetition
5. privilege   priviledge
6. definitely   definately
7. seperate   separate
8. desireable   desirable
9. development   developement
10. existence   existance
11. grammer   grammar
12. arguement   argument
13. surprise   supprise

Communicate with Quality

14.	achieve	acheive
15.	annoint	anoint
16.	tommorow	tomorrow
17.	irresistible	irresistable
18.	consensus	concensus
19.	accomodate	accommodate
20.	occurence	occurrence
21.	conscience	concience
22.	commitment	committment
23.	embarass	embarrass
24.	indispensible	indispensable
25.	allotted	alloted
26.	liaison	liason
27.	procede	proceed
28.	harrass	harass
29.	perseverance	perseverence
30.	ecstasy	ecstacy
31.	antequated	antiquated
32.	insistant	insistent
33.	exhilarate	exillarate

Communicate with Quality

34.	vacuum	vaccuum
35.	rediculous	ridiculous
36.	dictionery	dictionary
37.	oscillate	oscilate
38.	tyrannous	tyranous
39.	drunkeness	drunkenness
40.	dissention	dissension
41.	connoisseur	conoisseur
42.	sacrilegious	sacreligious
43.	batallion	battalion
44.	perogative	prerogative
45.	iridescent	irridescent
46.	inadvertent	inadvertant
47.	geneology	genealogy
48.	villify	vilify
49.	inoculate	innoculate
50.	dilettante	dilletante

Once a word has been allowed to escape, it cannot be recalled. —Horace

Communicate with Quality

15 Spelling Rules

It will probably help if you make your own list of spelling demons. Keep it near your desk and refer to it when necessary. Spell your demon words with the troublesome part in capital letters. (Chances are, it's not the whole word which is difficult for you, but rather just one syllable.)

Take a mental picture of the word with the upper-case syllable:

Wed-NES-day.

Refer to the list often. In time, your mind will supply you with the correct spelling and you won't need the list at all.

Here are some rules that may help your orthographical efforts.

1. The letter "y" preceded by a consonant becomes "i" before a suffix.

    ready - readily   fancy - fanciest   pretty - prettier

Of course, there are some exceptions to this rule:

    Keep the "y" to avoid a double "i."
        fly - flying (not fliing)

    Keep the "y" with certain one-syllable words.
        fly - flyer

2. If the "y" at the end of a word has a vowel in front of it, you will keep the 'y' when adding suffixes.

    monkey - monkeys

    <u>Exceptions</u>: lay - laid   pay - paid

He that hath knowledge spareth his words.   *Proverbs 17:27*

3. **When adding a suffix beginning with a vowel or with "y," drop the final "e."**

    love - lovable   whine - whining   brave - bravest

    Keep the "e" when the suffix begins with a consonant:
        home - homeliness   hope - hopeful   care - careless

4. **Form the plural of most nouns by adding an "s" to the singular.**

    boy - boys   road - roads   table - tables   meeting - meetings

5. **With single-syllable words, add "es" if the plural creates a new syllable.**

    box - boxes   watch - watches

6. **Words that end in "s" or an "s" sound form their plural by adding "es."**

    witness - witnesses   address - addresses   wish - wishes

7. **Certain words ending in "f" or "fe" drop these endings in the plural and add "ves" instead.**

    hoof - hooves   life – lives   knife - knives

8. **Most nouns ending in "o" in the singular have "es" added to form the plural.**

    hero - heroes   tomato - tomatoes

9. **Words ending in an "o" preceded by a vowel form their plural just by adding "s'.**

    radio - radios   studio - studios

10. **With compound words, add "s" to the final syllable.**

spoonful - spoonfuls   mouthful - mouthfuls

11. With compound words that are hyphenated, form the plural by adding "s" to the first word.

mother-in-law   -   mothers-in-law

12. With titles composed of more than one word, pluralize the important word.

Attorney General - Attorneys General

13. To show the plural of numbers or abbreviations or symbols, add an apostrophe plus "s" to avoid confusion.

a - a's   3 - 3's   # - #'s   SF171 - SF171's

14. For one-syllable words or words with an accented last syllable, double the final consonant before adding a vowel suffix if that final consonant is directly preceded by one vowel.

stop - stopped   permit - permitted   compel - compelled

15. Latin words ending in "um" or "us" form their plural by substituting these suffixes with "a" and "i" respectively.

datum - data   memorandum - memoranda   erratum - errata
alumnus - alumni   octopus - octopi   stimulus - stimuli   fungus - fungi

This will never be a civilized country until we expend more money for books than we do for chewing gum.   --Elbert Hubbard

Communicate with Quality

Closely related to spelling rules are rules governing the use of the hyphen. Here are some guidelines.

13 Rules for Using Hyphens

1. **Divide a word between syllables only.**

    be - tween

2. **Never divide a one-syllable word.**

    one

3. **Divide compound words at the hyphen.**

    one-syllable

4. **Do not divide a word of five letters or less, even if that word has more than one syllable.**

    even

5. **If possible, do not separate a one-letter syllable or two-letter syllable at the beginning from the rest of the word.**

    not hy-phenation but rather hyphen-ation

6. **If possible, do not separate a one-letter syllable or two-letter syllable at the end from the rest of the word.**

    not whenev-er but rather when-ever

7. **Divide words with a double final consonant at the double letters.**

    let-ters   sit-ting

8. Do not divide between double consonants that form the ending of a root word.

    not swel-ling but rather swell-ing

9. Hyphenate compound numbers from twenty-one to ninety-nine.

    twenty-two

10. When several words function as a single descriptor of a noun, those words are hyphenated.

    state-of-the-art equipment   high-velocity hammer

11. Certain prefixes are usually hyphenated.

    ex-wife   all-American   self-expression   semi-retired

12. If a prefix ends in a vowel and the word begins with the same vowel, use the hyphen to enhance readability.

    not reelected but rather re-elected

13. Use the hyphen to avoid confusion.

    recover (pertaining to health)
    re-cover (pertaining to furniture)

Just get it down on paper, and then we'll see what to do with it.
                                                --Maxwell Perkins

Communicate with Quality

Ameliorating Your Affect towards Lexical Acquisition:

Tautologies

People who are careless with their expression tend to use too many words. When an expression contains unnecessary verbiage or restates what need not be said, we call that expression a tautology. Here are some examples of tautological expressions. Can you think of others?

written correspondence	modern fashions of today
It's raining outside.	real people
I was thinking in my head.	past history
I saw it with my own eyes.	logical consequence
spoken conversation	wooly sheep
new innovation	salty brine
qualified expert	rubber tire
tuna fish	colorful rainbow
hot water heater	wander aimlessly
free gift	monogrammed initials
rounded curve	winding curve
straight line	circled around
true love	waving in the air
true confession	unsold inventory

Chapter 3: The Editing Process

16 Marks of Punctuation

The following familiar marks of punctuation, along with rules for their usage, are presented for your review. Study them carefully, for a diagnostic test follows.

- **Period**
    at the end of a sentence
    as a decimal point
    with abbreviations

? **Question Mark**
    after a sentence asking a question

! **Exclamation Point**
    with a statement of strong emotion or surprise (seldom used in business writing)

, **Comma**
    with words in a series
    before and after the name of a person being addressed
    before a conjunction (but, and) to join two complete thoughts
    to set off interrupters
    with appositives
    to set off nonrestrictive clauses (without which the sentences can still be understood)
    after introductory elements
    with certain abbreviations (such as Jr.)
    with dates

Communicate with Quality

       to separate city and state
       to separate quotations

;   **Semicolon**
       to join two complete thoughts
       for clarity when there are too many internal commas

:   **Colon**
       when the second half of the sentence illustrates the point made in the first half
       for enumerating after a complete thought
       for ratios and analogies

...   **Ellipsis**
       to indicate omissions

*   **Asterisk**
       to emphasize information

( )   **Parenthesis**
       with words that clarify
       to identify information sources

_ _   **Dash**
       with interrupting phrases

" "   **Quotation Marks**
       with quoted matter
       with certain titles
       for emphasis

'   **Apostrophe**
       for a quotation within a quotation
       for possession
       for contractions
       for pluralization of unique expressions

_   **Hyphen**
       for syllabification
       with compounds

when multiple words function as a single descriptor
to separate maiden and married names

[ ] **Brackets**
for a parenthetical thought within a parenthetical thought
for editorial comments [sic]

/ **Virgule**
to separate numerals in a date
to indicate option for the reader

_ **Underline**
with certain titles
for emphasis

The English language is rich with options. There are millions of words to choose from, some with the most subtle variations in meanings. And there are millions of combinations we can use to persuade, impress, inform, entertain, share experiences, write a scientific paper, accept a Nobel Prize, compose a romantic novel or leave a funny note for the paper boy.
--Jack Thomas

Communicate with Quality

Diagnostic Test: Punctuation

Having studied the marks of punctuation on the preceding pages, apply those rules to the following statements. Decide if the bracketed space needs a punctuation mark. If it does not, write "0" in the blank. If the bracketed space <u>does</u> need a mark, write the correct mark(s) in the space.

1. _____ Any boss [ ] who gives expensive Christmas gifts [ ] will be popular.

2. _____ "Are you [ ]" she demanded [ ] "the one in charge [   ]

3. _____ George Bush [ ] President of the United States [ ] addressed the Business Roundtable yesterday.

4. _____ The trainers' network [ ] which has an international membership [ ] provides many opportunities for self-growth.

5. _____ While the year [ ] end report was being prepared [ ] the meeting was in progress.

6. _____ She is definitely a "tweener [   ]

7. _____ Mr. McHugh contacted the members of each division to schedule a meeting [ ]

8. _____ Do you know any "dinks [   ]

9. _____ "Fire [   ] she shouted [ ]

10. _____ I need [ ] Mr. Jones [ ] a new desk, a new typewriter [ ] and a new desk chair.

11. _____ June is [ ] without a doubt [ ] the most accurate typist [ ] in the department.

12. _____ Therefore [ ] I think we should consider a Southern state again next year [ ] the planning committee concurs with my opinion.

13. _____ The organization of the firm is quite simple [ ] everyone

Communicate with Quality

reports to Mr. Jones.

14._____ Mr. Henry will use the famous [ ] "I have a dream [ ] line in his remarks tonight.

15._____ The names of the committee members are [ ] Lynette Day [ ] EEO Officer [ ] Susan Black [ ] Vice President in Charge of International Trade [ ] and Anthony Trollop [ ] Public Relations Officer.

16._____ The fixed-price proposal [ ] see Appendix II [ ] incorporates the manufacturing changes [ ] required to produce the component.

17._____ Mr. Fujitani [ ] despite what you may think [ ] is actually the most committed member of the team.

18._____ His article [ ] The Impact of Interim Funding [ ] will appear in the *Subcontractors Quarterly*.

19._____ She asks everyone [ ] Have you read Browning's poem [ ] How Do I Love Thee[ ]

20._____ The women[ ]s team has a better record than does the men[ ]s team.

21._____ He once wrote a letter to the Prince of Whales [ ] sic [ ] .

22._____ She has visited the site of Matthew Arnold's poem [ ] Dover Beach [ ]

23._____ The bar graph [ ] see page 14 [ ] depicts the escalation in our operating costs [ ] over the past twelve months.

24._____ The entire department [ ] all 16 of us [ ] is planning to take some vacation time during the month of June.

25._____ Optometrist[ ]s are the "apples of my eye. [ ]

Good writing and good speaking are simply the external aspects of good thinking.
--Ernest L. Boyer (former U. S. Commissioner of Education)

Communicate with Quality

10 Capitalization Rules

1. Capitalize the first word of a sentence, the first word of a direct quotation, the first word of a line of poetry, and the first word in outline categories.

Our office met its sales quota.

She asked, "Did you enclose the brochure?"

I'm nobody.
Who are you?
Are you
Nobody too?
    --Emily Dickinson

  I. Reports required
     A. Variance
     B. Activity
     C. Capital expenditure

2. Capitalize the first, last, and other important words in a title.

A Book of Days for the Literary Year

3. Capitalize proper nouns and their related adjectives.

France, French   Hebrew, Hebraic   Christian, Christianity

Do not capitalize such words if they have become part of familiar everyday expressions: plaster of paris   french fries
body english

4. Capitalize geographic regions but not compass directions.

He left the South and headed west until he reached California.

5. Capitalize nouns that have been personified.

Communicate with Quality

Mother Nature   Father Time   Old Man River

6. **Capitalize the pronoun "I."**

7. **Capitalize the first letter of abbreviated words.**
U.S.A.   Mr.   Dr.   Jr.   Ed. D.

8. **Capitalize the first word and all nouns in the salutation of a letter; capitalize the first word only in the complimentary closing.**

Dear Mr. Jones   Yours truly,

9. **Capitalize a title preceding a name.**

Dean Howard   Prime Minister Thatcher

10. **Capitalize the word depicting a family member when the word is used in direct address.**

How are you, Aunt Mary?

(You would not capitalize the word "aunt" in this sentence: Mary Thomas is my aunt.)

Writing is a solitary occupation. Family, friends, and society are the natural enemies of a writer. He must be alone, uninterrupted, and slightly savage if he is to sustain and complete an undertaking.   --Lawrence Clark Powell

Communicate with Quality

Diagnostic Test: Capitalization

If the boldface word or phrase is correctly written, write "O" in the blank space. If you feel the boldface word is written incorrectly, write "1" in the blank space.

1. _____ My **Sister** lives in Oneonta, New York.

2. _____ Mr. Thomas is a **college** graduate.

3. _____ In fact, he graduated from **Stanford university.**

4. _____ He whispered, "**don't** forget to mention the long-range goals."

5. _____ To reach our Torrance office, you have to head **south.**

6. _____ Sue, Mr. Boppart's secretary, was a **History** major.

7. _____ Do you have any information, **uncle** Joe, about mergers?

8. _____ Her letter began "**To Whom It May Concern.**"

9. _____ Hemingway's most famous book may well be *For Whom The Bell Tolls.*

10. _____ Should we order **chinese** food for the managers meeting?

11. _____ Most children like hamburgers and **French** fries.

12. _____ The national parks will be popular attractions this **Summer.**

13. _____ Harry Williams, **administrative assistant** to Ms. Bethany, has applied for a transfer to our Oakland location.

14. _____ "Have you finished the budget?" **He** asked.

Your manuscript is both good and original, but the part that is good is not original and the part that is original is not good.   --Samuel Johnson

48

Communicate with Quality

15._____ One of the most famous **avenues** in the world is Pennsylvania Avenue.

16._____ I spoke to Shari -- **What** is her last name? -- in the conference room just a minute ago.

17._____ In my **senior** year, I switched my major to philosophy.

18._____ He always works on his **monthly** report on Mondays.

19._____ This building is a Jewish **Synagogue.**

20._____ George is **president** of the local Toastmasters Club.

21._____ The **bible** is one of the best-selling books in the world.

22._____ It is the policy of this **company** to abide by government regulations.

23._____ In college I studied French, Russian, and **Accounting.**

24._____ The company will hold its annual picnic on the **fourth** of July.

25._____ The complimentary closing contained these words: **Yours Truly.**

The man who does not read good books has no advantage over the man who can't read them.   *--Mark Twain*

Communicate with Quality

Diagnostic Test: Capitalization and Punctuation

If you can find an error in these sentences, go right ahead and correct it!

1. It was his first trip to the far east.

2. Susans notes are much more thorough than your's.

3. Mr. Tompkins luggage was lost in San francisco twenty four days ago.

4. Im planning to spend Memorial Day in Reno, Nevada or El paso, Texas.

5. He said I agree. I am convinced the plan would never work.

6. Hal boasted our quality circle can do any job given to us.

7. Next Summer I plan to take more after hours classes.

8. His sons in laws business is doing very well.

9. Mr. Oliver Ruskuff jr. will join our team next week.

10. The ladies room is on the Third Floor.

11. As war strode across the stage, peace cowered in fear.

12. I believe you will enjoy reading the new annual report.

13. In the latest issue of Defense News is an article on leadership styles.

14. I heard her say yes Mr. Johnson. I'll be right there.

15. The house armed services committee has reduced the funding in this fiscal year.

Look out how you use proud words. When you let proud words go, it is not easy to call them back. They wear long boots, hard boots. --Carl Sandburg

Syntax Concepts

"Syntax" merely means the way words are put together to form a sentence. A solid understanding of syntactical concepts will help you edit your work more confidently.

Pronouns

As far as these pronouns are concerned, there are only two things to remember:

Subject Case	Object Case
I	me
He	him
She	her
We	us
They	them

1. When the verb in a sentence is a weak verb, you must use a subject case pronoun. (Weak verbs are any form of the verb "to be": am, is, are, was, were, will be, can be, might be (et cetera); has been, had been, could have been (et cetera).

    This is he.   The new councilwoman will be she.

2. When a pronoun is used in a prepositional phrase, the pronoun must be in the object case. (These are the most often used prepositions: about, above, across, after, against, along, amid, among, around, at, before, behind, below, beneath, beside, between, beyond, but, by, concerning, down, during, except, for, from, in, into, like, of, off, on, over, past, since, through, throughout, to, toward, under, until, unto, up, upon, with, within, without.)

    Susan gave the report to Joe and her.

Communicate with Quality

Parallelism

The careful business writer will make certain that a list of two or more elements is written in a consistent fashion. It doesn't matter how that list begins; it only matters that the items in the list are written with a parallel construction.

It would be wrong to say, "I like to swim, to read, and bowling." Instead, the sentence should read, "I like to swim, to read, and to bowl."

Diagnostic Test: Pronouns and Parallelism

Decide if the following sentences are correct as written. If so, place a "0" in the blank space. If you believe a particular sentence is not correct, place a "1" in the blank space and determine what the correct expression should be.

1. _____ Ms. Taylor told Tammy and I to complete the analysis.

2. _____ Between you and I, there is a strong sense of loyalty here.

3. _____ I predict the next general manager will be she.

4. _____ We would be behind schedule without Lundy and he.

5. _____ It will be them who begin to complain about the raises.

6. _____ The one who raised all that money was him.

7. _____ Mr. Brizend distributed the reports to we engineers.

8. _____ In the past, the culprits have been them.

9. _____ I heard the boss sent out a memo about you and I and the work we have done with the Adopt-a-School Program.

Communicate with Quality

10._____ Mr. Thompson talked about John and she.

11._____ She is skilled at typing, editing, and the placement of classified material into appropriate folders.

12._____ To finish a task on time is better than postponing it.

13._____ I need you to design the format, enter the data, and the distribution of copies to all who need to know.

14._____ This model has the following features: economical, durable, and simplicity of operation.

15._____ She shared not only her career goals with me but also wanting to move to a less congested area of the state.

16._____ You will find him cooperative, productive, sincere, and he is always on time.

17._____ During my five years at the hotel, I advanced from bottle-washer to innkeeping.

18._____ The awards are made to large businesses, small businesses, minority businesses, and to women who own their own businesses.

19._____ The negotiating process should include these considerations: the competitiveness of prices, delivery schedule, terms, and determining all the conditions.

20._____ The purpose of this letter is to detail the current status of outstanding charges and the suggestion of possible resolutions.

No one can write decently who is distrustful of the reader's intelligence or whose attitude is patronizing.   --E. B. White

Communicate with Quality

Indefinite Antecedent

The precise writer offers such clarity that there is no need for the reader to guess at the intended meaning of the communication. The careless writer, by contrast, may provide an expression which causes the reader to have more than one interpretation. If, for example, the careless writer uses a pronoun which may refer to more than one person, the reader will be confused. When that referent or antecedent is not made definite, the resulting problem is called "indefinite antecedent."

Look at this example:

    Jack showed Mr. Eason the letter he had written.

It is possible that Mr. Eason wrote the letter. However, it is also possible that Jack wrote the letter. The antecedent of the pronoun "he" is simply not clear or definite.

In the following sentences, draw arrows to the two possible antecedents of the underlined pronouns.

1. After the Senator watched the lion perform, <u>he</u> was fed 25 pounds of raw meat.

2. Hostility and aggression can be destructive to you and your family members. You must get rid of <u>them</u>.

3. You have many skills that are valuable to employers, so be sure to take advantage of <u>them</u>.

4. Two years ago, a mole appeared on my nose, <u>which</u> I decided to have surgically removed.

5. A truck ran off the winding road and struck the telephone pole as <u>it</u> tried to get back onto the paved surface.

6. She admired his muscular biceps as <u>they</u> nodded to one another by the registration desk.

Communicate with Quality

7. Burglars stole a television from the car of Mrs. Loretta Kunkle even though her husband was in <u>it.</u>

8. The Air Force pilots were impressed by the waves as <u>they</u> crashed on the rocks.

9. Individuals who employ birth control techniques <u>that</u> smoke frequently run the risk of having retarded children.

10. Mrs. Jeffries will have her cat's tail operated on, but if it fails to heal properly, <u>she</u> will have to be put away.

Misplaced Modifiers

As an effective business writer, you must make certain that your modifying words are near the person or thing they are modifying. If they are not, your reader may misunderstand your meaning.

Which of these two sentences is correct?

>Hanging from a vine, the monkey was able to escape from the rhino.
>Hanging from a vine, the rhino was unable to pursue the monkey.

Clearly, the first sentence is the correct one, as it has the modifying phrase "hanging from a vine" near the noun it is modifying: "monkey."

Underline the correct sentence in each pair.

1. Being correctly typed, the boss appreciated my report.
   Being correctly typed, my report evoked the boss' appreciation.

2. Walking rapidly down the hall, a noise startled me.
   Walking rapidly down the hall, I was startled by a noise.

3. Being old and decrepit, I was able to buy the house for a low price.
   Being old and decrepit, the house sold for a low price.

Communicate with Quality

4. Tired and depressed, quitting seemed the only available option.
   Tired and depressed, he regarded quitting as the only available option.

5. Confused by the freeway signs, the exit ramp was missed.
   Confused by the freeway signs, she missed the exit ramp.

6. Singing her favorite song, her bicycle sped down the street.
   Singing her favorite song, the girl sped down the street on her bicycle.

7. Caught up in playing political games, alienation from her peers was the result.
   Caught up in playing political games, the woman alienated her peers.

8. Reading a mystery novel, the sound of a scream made him panic.
   Reading a mystery novel, the man panicked at the sound of a scream.

9. Striding into the boss' office, I demanded to see the report.
   Striding into the boss' office, the report was what I demanded to see.

10. Trapped by her constant chattering, I decided to be rude.
    Trapped by her constant chattering, rudeness seemed my only choice.

11. Traveling in Europe, I was amazed by the number of polyglots.
    Traveling in Europe, the number of polyglots amazed me.

12. Using the Berkoff Blastoff, we saw David Berkoff take the lead.
    Using the Berkoff Blastoff, David Berkoff took the lead.

13. After being featured on *Your Hit Parade*, Frank Sinatra's fans multiplied.
    After being featured on *Your Hit Parade*, Frank Sinatra became more popular than ever with his fans.

14. I found this report going through my drawers.
    While going through my drawers, I found this report.

15. Staring out the window, the cityscape looked intriguing.
    Staring out the window, the man found the cityscape intriguing.

The grammatical man leads a logical life.   --Anonymous

Communicate with Quality

Ameliorating Your Affect towards Lexical Acquisition

Antonyms

In the blank space, write the antonym (word that means the opposite) for each of the following. Each antonym must begin, as does the one in the example, with the letter "s."

Example: ___sister___ brother.   Starting time: _____

1. _____ cheerful   _____ choose
2. _____ fool   _____ terse
3. _____ purchase   _____ double
4. _____ undefined   _____ delicate
5. _____ irrationality   _____ flourish
6. _____ disgusting   _____ assembled
7. _____ sufficient   _____ hide
8. _____ smile   _____ accept
9. _____ calligraphy   _____ virtue
10. _____ unethical   _____ benevolence

Ending time: _____

Success comes to a writer, as a rule, so gradually that it is always something of a shock to him to look back and realize the heights to which he has climbed.
--P. G. Wodehouse

Communicate with Quality

Chapter 4: The Proofreading Process

12 Proofreading Techniques

1. Read Backwards

If you had hoped this section would provide you with shortcuts to proofreading, you will be disappointed. If anything, this section will encourage you to take even <u>more</u> time as you read your final copy, looking for errors. The reading-backwards technique should be done after you have read the document the usual way the first time. The usual reading, however, may cause you to overlook errors since you are so familiar with the content of the material. The proximity of related ideas sometimes causes us to skip right over our errors. When we are caught up with the meaning of the words, the orderly progression of points can prevent us from spotting obvious mistakes.

When you read backwards -- starting with the very last word at the bottom of the page and then moving up, line by line, reading from right to left instead of left to right -- you will be looking at words by themselves. Since the backwards approach forces us to look at separate words and not at the logical flow of ideas, we can catch more typographical errors.

Read the following lines aloud. Then read them a second time -- backwards.

PARIS	A BIRD	ONCE
IN THE	IN THE	UPON A
THE SPRINGTIME	THE HAND	A TIME

With the second, "backwards" reading, you probably caught the double

Communicate with Quality

words that you may have missed the first time around. Our eyes truly can play tricks upon us. Two people may be looking at the identical image, yet each might have a different impression. What do <u>you</u> see in the following: an old woman, a young woman, or both?

Try your new techniques here. Read the eight-line paragraph on the next page the regular way, counting how many times the letter "f" appears. Record here the number of times you saw the letter "f." _____

Then read the passage backwards, starting with the word "management" at the very end and continuing to the word "The" at the very beginning. How many times did you count the letter "f" in your second reading? _____

Communicate with Quality

1. The need for training foremen of first-class factories in the careful
2. handling of factory paraphernalia is foremost in the minds of facto-
3. ry owners. Since the forefathers of the factory owners trained fore-
4. men for first-class factories in the careful handling of factory
5. paraphernalia, the factory owners feel they should carry on with
6. the family tradition of training foremen of first-class factories in
7. the handling of factory paraphernalia because they believe it is the
8. basis of fundamental factory management.

Here are some other proofreading techniques which should help you achieve excellence in both the content and the context of your documents.

2. Read aloud, pronouncing every single syllable.

3. Have a partner read your typed copy while you listen and compare it to the original.

4. Double check your citations. If the text refers you to page 42 in an appendix, turn to page 42 to see if the referenced page number is correct.

5. Check for format consistency (including pagination and enumerations) before beginning to read the words.

6. If possible, put the document aside for a while and come back to it later that day or even the next day. Proofread it again with a fresh, concentrated effort.

7. Turn the page upside down and scan it quickly to see if there is consistency in the format and in the spacing, especially where headlines are used.

8. Check dates. Look at a calendar to be certain the dates are accurately listed. If the communication is typed in January, make certain you have the new year listed and not the old one which you have been using for twelve months.

Communicate with Quality

9. Whenever you are interrupted, place a light check mark next to the last word you typed. When you return to that page, continue from the check mark and don't worry about having typed the same line(s) twice or having omitted whole sections.

10. If the originator has handed you a fragmented document with many inserts and many scraps of paper, number the paragraphs. Then go back after typing and check to see that your typed version has the same number of paragraphs as in the original.

11. Make a style sheet to help ensure consistency.

12. When typing columns of numbers, fold the original and place it beside the column you typed. It's easier to check numbers when they are right next to each other.

Exercise #1

You may find it hard to believe, but the following letter was actually received by a businessman who had written to a major California bank, trying to straighten out a problem with his Master Card. How many errors can you find?

1. WE try to solve your problem regarding ordering New M/CH. We can not
2. reorder a new one ,because You have a foreing adress.

3. Once You supplies the Bank with a loco adress, there wont be any
4. problem.

5. WE credited your account with double billing of $21.87, and that
6. amount will show as credit on your nex statement.

7. I checked your statement mailing adress last year and it show P. O. Box
8. number. My be also this time you can still used it.

9. Please let me kno about it. I realy would like to solve your problem
10. complitly to your satisfaction.

Communicate with Quality

11. Hope to hear from You soon,

12. Fondly,

Exercise #2

Here are other error-filled statements which actually appeared in print. What should be done to correct each error?

a. Help Wanted: sadistical secretary

b. Go to your nearest dealer and inquire about RCA living colon. They will be glad to give you a free demonstration.

c. Do in yourself and make a first-class job.

d. Tired of cleaning yourself? Let me do it for you. My rates are very fair.

e. He had his girl fried with him on his trip south.

f. He studied unclear physics at the Massachusetts Institute of Technology.

g. For sale: light green, strapless formal. Whoops included.

h. Nikita Khrushchev will visit West Point and the United States Nasal Academy.

i. Try Chesterfields if you really want a good choke.

j. We have received a new shipment of Arrow shirts for men with l6 necks.

k. Mr. Sitlow is recovering from a head injury and shock caused by coming in contact with a live wife.

l. In Chicago, six men have been accused of bride-taking.

Communicate with Quality

m. Last week we said Mr. Oglem is a defective in the police force. We meant, of course, a detective in the police farce.

n. Mr. Kevin Harrison undressed the D.A.R. Tuesday afternoon.

o. Richard Green is playing his old position of right tickle.

Exercise #3

Not just journalists are guilty of typographical errors. While less amusing and less obvious, there are errors in each of the following. Can you spot them?

1. Each of us in the Accounting Department look forward to meeting you and welcome you to our organization.

2. To maximize our efforts, the conference room will be reserved for the entire day.

3. The rationale being that an informal atmosphere is most conducive to cooperation and brainstorming on this project.

4. We are anxious to discuss with you: monitoring the number of rejects, overseeing the clerical staff, budgeting for training, and the implementation of employee's suggestions.

5. The concensus of opinion seems to be: a need for more group activities, a need for better communication, and a need for more release time.

Exercise #4

Film producer Samuel Goldwyn was (in)famous for verbicide, the distortion of language. You may enjoy reading his erroneous expressions.

a. Let's have some new cliches.

Communicate with Quality

b. Anyone who goes to a psychiatrist should have his head examined.

c. A verbal contract isn't worth the paper it's written on.

d. First you have a good story, then a good treatment, and next, a first-rate director. After that, you hire a competent cast and even then you have only the mucus of a good picture.

e. I'll give you a definite maybe.

f. I had a great idea this morning, but I didn't like it.

g. The only trouble with this business is the dearth of bad pictures.

h. Let's bring it up-to-date with some snappy 19th Century dialogue.

i. We've got 25 years' worth of files out there, just sitting around. Now what I want you to do is to go out there and throw everything out -- but make a copy of everything first.

j. Now why did you name your baby John? Every Tom, Dick, and Harry is named John.

k. In two words: im-possible.

l. Include me out.

m. I read part of it all the way through.

Exercise #5

With this practice exercise, you will have a chance to proofread numbers. It's easiest to work with a partner on this kind of statistical proofreading. However, you can also achieve excellent results with the paper-folding method mentioned on page 61. If you are working by yourself, read the numbers aloud as you check them. This use of multiple senses helps insure accuracy. As an alternative, you may find a ruler or other straight-

Communicate with Quality

edged tool beneficial. When possible, cover up the other columns of numbers to help focus your attention on the one column you are reading.

Regard the figures on the left as the ones you typed; the data on the right represent the correct figures on which you based the report. Can you find all 18 errors?

FUND-RAISING INCOME: 1991 Actual and 1992 Goal			**FUND-RAISING INCOME:** 1991 Actual and 1992 Goal		
Branch	1991	1992	Branch	1991	1992
1	100	135	1	100	135
2	96	149	2	86	149
3	541	519	3	441	519
4	294	301	4	294	302
5	195	207	5	195	207
6	218	489	6	218	489
6	521	608	7	521	608
7	419	567	8	419	567
8	128	216	9	128	316
9	392	428	10	392	428
10	447	449	11	447	449
11	291	379	12	291	339
12	281	598	13	281	589
13	75	167	14	72	167
14	283	388	15	283	388
16	851	976	16	851	976
17	1001	988	17	1000	988
18	325	326	18	325	326

Communicate with Quality

Exercise #6

We can often improve the integrity of a document by bringing precision and concision to the syntax. Bring clarity to the following real-world sentences by streamlining: eliminate unnecessary words, use strong action verbs in place of weak ones, and reduce the number of prepositional phrases.

a. If the proposal is rejected by your office, clear and logical reasons must be submitted in sufficient detail to permit transmittal to the proposer, without editing or revision being needed.

_____

_____

_____

b. A discussion with the proposer and you, the supervisor, is encouraged where feasible during or after the evaluation of the proposal. A useful purpose can be accomplished if such discussions are employed by the supervisor and his or her subordinate, in order that they can be used to convey the company's interest in both the proposal of the given employee, as well as its interest in the program itself.

_____

_____

_____

_____

c. A suspense date of evaluation for local adoption, rejection, or forwarding to higher authority has been established; that date is April 30, 1994. If this date cannot be met, this office should be notified and an interim reply as to a target date for completion should be given to replace the specified date of April 30, 1994.

d. Please insure that an information copy of each transmittal document forwarding the suggestion to the various levels and activities is furnished to the individuals whose names are listed below. This will enable us to insure that the proposer is kept well-informed of the progress of the proposal which has been submitted.

e. It is the purpose of this article to report on the state of the parks in this state which are the subject of controversy between environmentalists and some government officials because of the way the parks are being handled and because of the widespread and complex problems which seem to be the result of lack of foresight.

f.   There are many causes and the possibility of many cures for the crisis which is the major concern of authorities who have reported the identification of 4,345 threats to park resources in a report that was entitled "State of the Parks" and which was presented in Congress in the year 1988.

_____

_____

_____

_____

Exercise #7

The following letter is yet another example of the drivel and dross which actually pass for correspondence from some firms. In this case, all identifying information has been omitted to protect the guilty. Correct all the errors you can find.

1.   As per your request I am writting this letter to explain the reason
2.   rats have apreared at the newly constructed building located at
3.   6723.

4.   Newly contructed byildings have a tendency to have rodents due to
5.   the fact the construction workers leave food around. The dirt
6.   surrounding the building is distrubed and the rodents burrough in the
7.   groud come out, and try and find a new home. Landscaping, new
8.   vegetation is inviting for the rodents.

9.   We have placed bait, traps, bait stations, glue and have made many
10. trips to crub this new infestation. We happy to report that many
11. dead rodents have been killed and everything possible is being done
12. to eliminate the problem.

13. Please be patient and when all the holes or openings are sealed the
14. rodents will be gone.

15. If there are any questions please do not hesitate to call. Thank you
16. for all the cooperation you have extended us in the past.

Exercise #8

Read and correct all the errors you can find in this article written by Sharon L. Renda, President; Janet M. Rosenberger, Personnel Consultant; and Diane M. Hall, Personnel Consultant at Renda Personnel Consultants, Inc. (Note: the errors did not appear in the original; they were inserted as a proofreading exercise.) Reprinted with permission of the authors.

Secretarial: The Respected Career of Today and Tomorrow

1) Over and over we read about the current and future shortage of qualified Secretaries. Theories point to the demands of the market far outweighing the supply of Baby Boomers, or to the women's movement encouraging higher degrees for managmeent positions, or to peer pressure to get a "real good job". The Secretary is often an underrated, underutilized person, striving for respect, believability and untimately credibility.

2) Being a Secretary -- a very good Secretary -- is a most important career in the business world today and tomorrow. But how do you get there? When do you know you have attained the level of credibility you have consistently tried to achieve in your secretarial career? For today's secretary, reaching the top means to earn believability on a short term basis and to gain credibility long term. This is not an overnight process, but rather one that evolves with time and patience. Whether you have a years experience of fifteen years' experience as a Secretary, the breaking-in period in any new secretarial position can be as much as six months to a year or longer, depending on you, your manager and the company. What it it takes to read the top is a multi-faceted process:

3) **TECHNICAL SKILLS** enable you to apply for the job. While these skils

may often represent only 25-50% of the job requirements, they are the foundation of a Secretary's position.

4) PRESENTATION enhances the technical skills and contributes to the success of the secretary. Finesse, attitude, personality, business and personal mannerisms, and appropriate grooming for the job are essential traits and should be maintained each and evey day on thejob.

5) **GOOD JUDGEMENT** often is not good enough. Today's business world demands excellant judgment. Tack, common sense and the ability to think on your feet comprise other cornerstones for the successful Secretary's career.

6) **Strong Written and Verbal Skills** enable a secretary to be an effective liaison for the manager and the co-workers and business clients of the company as well as the outside community. This will open opportunities to be supportive, creative and decision.

7) Time in the position and competence in these four areas will merge to make the Secretary an effective **TEAM PLAYER** with subordinates, superior and outsiders. A successful team-playing Secretary is unsselfish, takes pride in the manager and in the corporate goals and philosophies. It it is crucial to maintain the utmost confidentiality not only for the manager but for co-workers alike. Prima donas and power players are rarely tolerated, especially for the long haul. Willingness to learn from others, to accept criticism graciously and to be courteous, trustworthy and diplomatic -- these are intangibles a career Secretary will want to possess.

8) Blend all of these skils to attain **BELIEVABILITY** short term. Strive to improve, to learn and above all to be flexible enough to adapt to change. It is then that you can, with time, reach the ultimate goal--**CREDIBILITY.** Proving this "once" will not be enough. You have to earn respect, trust and responsibility with each new position.

9) How should you, as the career Secretary, perceive yourself? Consider yourself a professional and you in turn will be treated as a professional. Remember that Secretaries are responsible for supporting a manager's goals, ideas, and philosophies. The successful manager is often the reflection of an organized, supportive and capable Secretary.

10) A manager will respect the opinions and knowledge of the career Secretary and look for input in both daily activities and long term planning. The Secretary will be expected to take and interest in and share the triumphs and shortcomings of the manager. The Secretary who is supportive, loyal, and maintains confidentiality, while maintaining an accurate profile of her/his manager (all faults, all sides, the best and the worst) will achieve the ultimate credibility and loyalty desired.

11) A Secretary is a vital person in any organization and should be very proud of her/his important rule. The rewards and sense of accomplishment for the professional secretary are immeasurable. We know -- we have each been there ourselfs.

Exercise #9

In this exercise, you are asked to improve a document by formatting it. Use any or all of these typographical aids to enhance the readability of your document. (Always check for consistency when using these formatting devices.)

- white space
- bullets and other dingbats
- underlining
- indentation
- enumeration
- capital letters
- different fonts
- boldface print
- headlines
- italics
- different print sizes
- graphics
- charts
- subject line

This is the document your boss has presented to you, with the plea to make it as readable (and as accurate) as possible.

Communicate with Quality

Gentlemen;

1) This letter acknowleges ACME Companys' authorization of the $4,000 funding extended to Bieglow Company via the Acme letter #2-899-28, dated August 4, 1989, Acme letter #9-899-30, dated July 15, 1989, and the verbal agreement reached by Mssrs. Franklin Smith of Acme and Anthony Bigelow of Bigelow. Enclosed you will find Bigelow's acknowledgement of Purchase Order Revision (POR) No. 2 to Purchase Order #2812, Enclosure 1 which has been issued by Acme to provide additional funding to support the partial cost increase due to the Acme-directed changes, and the letter of intent which was written by Mr. Smith following the meeting with Mr. Bigelow.

2) Also enclosed is Bigelow's acknowledgement to POR #1 concerning Purchase Order #5123 which was issued by Acme to cancel Purchase Order #4122.

3) Since this POR #1 canceled the purchase order prior to the execution of Change Order #25C; we are also returning Change Order #25C unsigned.

4) If you have any questions, please do not hesitate to contact the undersigned at (213) 555-4631.

Exercise #10

Encircle the correct word for each sentence.

1. I will (accept/except) the assignment.

2. His retirement had a considerable (affect/effect) on staff morale.

3. My computer was more expensive than (her's/hers).

4. We went (passed/past) the exit this morning.

5. The duty of the legislature is to (affect/effect) the will of the people.

6. All the members were included (accept/except) Sue.

7. Were you (affected/effected) by the layoffs?

8. His (affect/effect) actually changes if he is deprived of sunshine.

9. Houdini was a great (allusion-/illusion-) ist.

10. Her (allusions/illusions) to her former boss were frequent.

11. Albany is the (capital/capitol) of New York.

12. You need (capital/capitol) to start your own business.

13. I will (choose/chose) the meeting place this afternoon.

14. You (choose/chose) an excellent candidate.

15. That scarf really (complements/compliments) your suit.

16. Mr. Smith paid his assistant quite a (complement/compliment).

17. Here are (complimentary/complementary) passes to the concert.

18. The Russian (emigrant/immigrant) defected while on tour.

19. The (eminent/imminent) meteorologist is on television.

20. He is saying that a storm is (eminent/imminent).

21. It is not the money -- it is the (principal/principle) that worries me.

22. I have (already/all ready) discussed this problem with you.

23. We have (all together/altogether) too many factions in the office.

24. Place the carton (beside/besides) the cabinet, if you will.

25. The vice presidents spoke to (there/they're/their) personnel.

Communicate with Quality

Exercise #11

In this penultimate test of your proofreading ability, you are asked to find all the mistakes you can in the following selections:

#1) My job is a highly-rewarding one. I am continuously challanged, and find I can effect the lives of others in some small way. My boss accomodates my requests whenever he can. Its rewarding for me to be able to show other employees' how their cooperative efforts can make a distinct difference in the company's over-all effort. I've been here twenty five years.

#2)   The specifics concerning the position are:

Experience	Salary Increment	Notification Date
1-3 years experiance	$4000	Monday, May 6
4-6 years experiance	$6000	Monday, May 13
6-9 years experiance	$8000	Monday, May 19

Exercise #12

Executive Orders <u>used</u> to begin, "By virtue of the authority vested in me by the Constitution of the United States of America, and as President of the United States of America, it is hereby ordered as follows...."

Cognizant of the time and money wasted by excess verbiage, however, the White House has revised the way Executive Orders are written. Today, they begin, "As President of the United States, I order...."

In the following exercise, you are asked to rewrite the passage so that its basically simply message can be more readily understood. Eliminate the pompous, unnecessary wording and get directly to the point.

> It was the nocturnal segment of the diurnal period preceding the annual celebratory observance of the emergence of a deified individual into the mundane environment, and throughout our

place of residence, kinetic activity was not in evidence among the possessors of this potential, including that species of domestic rodent known as Mus Musculus. Hosiery was meticulously suspended from the forward edge of the woodburning caloric apparatus, pursuant to our anticipatory pleasure regarding an imminent visitation from an eccentric philanthropist among whose folkloric appellations is the canonization of the figure whose agnomen has a rhyming association with the lead cantor from an assemblage known as the revolving petrous substances.

Additional Practice

Try simplifying these real-world examples.

1. Because of our continuing concern for employee security and subsequent to thorough reviews, Policy #254, which is entitled "Facility Security," was instated. In general, that which was intended has been accomplished, but not to the degree desired. Failures can be traced almost completely to laxity on the part of responsible supervisors and managers.

2. Notwithstanding any other provisions of this order, including but not limited to the provisions of the clauses of this order entitled "Changes" and "Termination," Seller shall not be bound to continue performance, incur costs or obligations or take any other action in connection with this order, including any changes thereto pursuant to the clause of this Order entitled "Changes," which would cause the total amount which Buyer would otherwise be obligated to pay Seller, in the event of completion, terminaation for convenience of Buyer pursuant to the clause hereunder entitled "Termination," or otherwise, to exceed the sum allotted then set forth in this Order.

In every man's writing, the character of the writer must lie recorded.
—Thomas Carlyle

Communicate with Quality

Commonly used Proofreading Symbols

1. Missing punctuation: ⋀

    Rochester, New York⋀is my hometown.

2. Incorrect punctuation: Cross out wrong mark; insert right one.

    Whenever I see Jane⨯ she is in a hurry.

3. Omit letter or word: / *or* ⨯

    Terry*y*/

4. Misspelled, mistyped or substituted words: Cross out wrong word; insert right one.

    Accommodations
    ~~Accomodations~~ were made for out-of-town visitors.

5. Capitalization: ≡

    The president and Mr. Quayle met with reporters today.

6. Lower case for a letter: /

    My boss was a /History major when he was in college.

7. Lower case for a whole word: /‾

    The /PURCHASE /ORDER was sent to Smith's by mistake.

8. Close a space: ◡

    The leasing reports were mis filed.

9. Reduce the number of spaces: ‿ *or* //

    Mr.‿Daniel Rathernot

Communicate with Quality

10. Insert a space: #

   The secretaries#were honored at a special luncheon.

11. Insert a missing word: ∧

   This is ∧*a* popular topic with researchers.

12. Show letters or words have been transposed: ∿

   Sacramento is the capital of Califo**rn**ia.

13. Delete: ⤴

   The Engineering Department ~~had~~ has two vacancies.

14. Leave as written (when used in the text): . . . .

   I found tho̤s̤e̤ books in the conference room.

15. Leave as written (when used in the margin): *stet*

16. Align: ⫽

   ⫽Mr. Thomas V. Jones
   ⫽ 555 Crenshaw Boulevard

17. Move right:]

18. Move left: [

19. Center horizontally:][

20. Indicate new paragraph: ¶

21. Indicate no new paragraph: *no* ¶

77

In the space provided, write the proofreading symbol called for.

1. Close a space   _____

2. Tranposed   _____

3. Delete   _____

4. Indicate a new paragraph   _____

5. Missing punctuation   _____

6. Lower case   _____

7. Insert a space   _____

8. Insert a missing word _____

9. Capitalization   _____

10. Incorrect punctuation _____

11. Move right   _____

12. Center horizontally   _____

13. Indicate no new paragraph _____

14. Move left   _____

15. Let it stand (for text)   _____

16. Let it stand (for margin) _____

17. Align   _____

Communicate with Quality

DOCUMENT CHECKLIST

Can you answer yes to the following questions about each communication you prepare?

COMPLETE

    a.   Does it provide all the information the reader will need to make a decision?
    b.   Has it anticipated any further questions or requests the reader may have?

CONCISE

    a.   Does it have a distinct, logical pattern of organization?
    b.   Have the proper words been chosen?
    c.   Is the point or purpose of the communication stated clearly at the beginning and then re-stated in the conclusion?
    d.   Is the language level matched to the reader(s)?
    e.   Are there transitions to link ideas together?

CORRECT

    a.   Is the information accurate?
    b.   Does the tone conform with professional practices?
    c.   Have all spelling, grammar, and/or punctuation questions been resolved?

APPROPRIATE

    a.   Is the style appropriate for this particular reader?
    b.   Have hackneyed phrases and jargon been removed?
    c.   Will this communication achieve its intended purpose?

Next to the originator of a good sentence is the first quoter of it.   --Emerson

Ameliorating Your Affect toward Lexical Acquisition

Kangaroo words

Certain words in our language are known as "kangaroo words," for they contain their actual synonym within their original spelling. The synonym is spelled with letters in exactly the same order as they appear in the original.

    <u>Example:</u> F-<u>E</u>-<u>A</u>-S-<u>T</u>   synonym: E-A-T

    He will <u>feast</u> on lobster. He will <u>eat</u> lobster.

Try finding the kangaroo words in each of the following.

1. hostel _____

2. deliberate (verb) _____

3. appropriate ("proper" is not the answer) _____

4. fabrication ("fabric" is not the answer) _____

5. precipitation _____

6. supervisor _____

7. catacomb _____

8. rotund _____

9. separate _____

10. facade _____

Can you think of others?

Communicate with Quality

Chapter 5: Telephone Tips and Techniques

Customer Service Considerations

A recent study by the Rockefeller Corporation found there were specific and perhaps surprising reasons why customers leave one business and turn to another for a desired product.

- 1%   do not return because they have died.
- 3%   turn away because they have moved to another area.
- 5%   leave because they have found a friend or acquaintance who can supply the product.
- 9%   have been won over by the competition.
- 14% find another company because they are dissatisfied with the product.

Subtotal: 32%   of customers are lost for the reasons listed above.

A full 68% of the remaining "lost" customers stop doing business with a given company because they feel the company simply does not care.

What happens when customers feel they have been treated poorly?
They tell other people about that treatment!

In a 1983 study, the Whirlpool Corporation found that in making purchasing decisions, Americans rely most heavily on the judgment of others. (40% of customers depended on other people as a reliable source of purchase decisions, as opposed to 6% who depended on print and electronic adver-advertising.) Now, when the word-of-mouth form of advertising is negative, some potentially disastrous results occur.

Communicate with Quality

Studying advertising strategies ("Measuring the Grapevine: Consumer Response and Word-of-Mouth"), the Coca Cola Company found that customers tell twice as many people about a negative experience as they tell about a positive experience. Further, 30% of consumers with a complaint that was not answered <u>never</u> return to the firm that was the source of that complaint.

Further eye-opening data about consumer reactions have been compiled by the Technical Assistance Research organization in Washington, D.C. They found that the average customer tells nine to sixteen friends about a bad experience she had; in some cases, customers tell more than 20 other people about poor treatment they received.

And, the Direct Sales Association has concluded that it costs five times as much to get a dissatisfied customer back as it costs to make him a customer in the first place.

So very often, treatment of a customer, at least initially, is determined by a phone call. When the caller feels her request or inquiry is handled professionally, she makes a subjective judgment about the firm being represented by the person on the other end of the phone line. A positive reaction leads to repeat business and favorable word-of-mouth recommendations.

Think about the last time you were treated unprofessionally by a telephone representative -- of your own company or of a different firm. Briefly describe the experience here.

_____

_____

_____

_____

_____

_____

Communicate with Quality

6 Telephone Horror Stories which Cost People Their Jobs or which Cost Companies Good Customer Relations

A senior vice president in a major Southern California aerospace firm called a manufacturing department for information. The person who answered the phone had recently been hired and therefore was not familiar with the names of executives in the upper echelon. The vice president began the conversation by stating, "This is John Smith."

To which the person at the other end of the line replied, "So?"

───────────────────────────

A very competent (but not especially grammatical) switchboard operator in a management firm received a call from a high-level official in the corporate office. The caller asked for the general manager of the management firm.

To which the switchboard operator replied, "He ain't done come back from lunch yet."

───────────────────────────

A caller to an entertainment industry firm asked for Miss Smith, a vice president in charge of production. The caller was told, "She's in the toilet."

───────────────────────────

An executive in a manufacturing firm called one of his production departments and was able to tell quickly that the person who picked up the phone did not have full command of the English language. Precious minutes were wasted as the executive tried to make clear the purpose of his call.

The foreign-born individual, no doubt feeling as much frustration as did the executive, finally explained, "No speak English!" and hung up the phone.

───────────────────────────

A caller to a real estate firm asked for a person in the Accounts Payable Department and was told, "Oh, she died last week."

Communicate with Quality

A caller (and potentially new customer) of a tax preparation firm asked to speak with the senior auditor.

To which the telephone operator replied, "Oh, he quit last week. He's the third person to quit this month. No one stays here very long."

———————————————————

Individual employees can create powerful impressions of the organization for which they work. That impression can be a negative one if the employee has not been trained to present the company well to both internal and external calls. If you are curious about how your firm is being represented, call from the outside with a question or complaint and see how well you are treated.

Are you and your co-workers projecting an image of professionalism and courtesy? Does the average caller hang up the phone feeling that he or she has been well treated? Do employees of your firm attempt to project a "wow factor," a feeling that the caller is indeed important to the firm?

Analyze your own telephone personality. (What specific behaviors of professionalism do you exhibit?) Then write a letter to your boss from someone with whom you typically deal on the phone. You will have to place yourself in that other person's shoes. Honestly assess your own telephone techniques and then write as if you were that other person.

———————————————————————————————

———————————————————————————————

———————————————————————————————

———————————————————————————————

———————————————————————————————

———————————————————————————————

———————————————————————————————

Communicate with Quality

30 Things to Avoid When on the Phone

1. chewing gum
2. inhaling deeply on a cigarette
3. not listening carefully
4. not recognizing voices of frequent callers
5. not being clear when presenting information
6. being rude
7. losing poise
8. eating food
9. shuffling papers or continuing to work at a keyboard
10. sounding bored
11. failing to use common sense
12. speaking too quickly or too slowly, too loudly or too softly
13. not knowing how to spell common words
14. laughing before beginning to speak
15. putting the caller on hold before she has had a chance to speak
16. being too poised
17. not sounding knowledgeable
18. asking the caller to repeat information, repeatedly
19. having a note of incredulity in your voice, as if the caller is doing something wrong or asking an improper question
20. speaking to someone else while on the line with the caller
21. drinking coffee or a soft drink loudly enough to be heard
22. relying on stock phrases ("Have a nice day.")
23. putting caller on hold for too long a period
24. cutting the person off
25. hanging up loudly
26. using a speaker phone

There are, of course, ever so many other transgressions of telephone etiquette. One that is particularly annoying is to have the operator assume you are 19 years old and address you as "Honey" or even "Baby Love."

What are other negative behaviors that you can add to this list? Confer with a partner and see if you can add at least four more.

27. _____

Communicate with Quality

28. _____

29. _____

30. _____

Here is a tip that may help you regard the telephone not as a source of interruption but rather as a source of opportunity: put a note on the phone that says, "It's my job calling." This written reminder of the importance of telephone communications (whether upwards, downwards, lateral, or external) will help you project a tone of concern for the caller.

Without "conscious" effort, we cannot improve the image we project over the phone. To develop that consciousness, pay careful attention over the next several weeks to three occasions on which you demonstrated either a very positive or a very negative image. Then analyze determining factors.

Situation #1

_____

_____

_____

_____

_____

Situation #2

_____

_____

Communicate with Quality

_____

_____

Situation #3

_____

_____

_____

_____

_____

_____

40 Tips for Projecting Professionalism

1.   Concentrate on the call. Give your fullest attention to the caller and listen carefully to what is being said. Do not be distracted by the environment. If necessary, control that environment before continuing the call.

2.   Have paper and pencil ready before you begin the call.

3.   Answer the phone properly. "Yeah?" is not an acceptable greeting, yet it is heard so often in the business world.

4.   Answer the phone promptly. A phone which rings and rings leaves the caller wondering what is happening on the other end of the line.

5.   Consider using an answering machine, if only for a specified period of time during the day. You will be freed to work without interruption. And -- believe it or not -- some callers prefer to state their message simply and then await a call back if necessary.

Communicate with Quality

6. Never put the person on hold without first finding out who the person is or what he or she needs. (The call may be an emergency call, for example, and valuable time could be wasted if the person is on hold.) You may wish to ask if the person would prefer to be called back or to be placed on hold.

7. Use body language to help you convey a receptive, welcoming tone. Actually shrug your shoulders before picking up the phone as a way of separating yourself from the work you are doing. Smile before you begin; many expert telephone users find this technique helps them establish and maintain a pleasant manner.

8. Make certain your tone of voice is professional, enthusiastic, and helpful. Do not sound bored, annoyed, or uncaring.

9. Obtain the person's name and use it during the conversation. (Galvanic skin responses show that a person's name is one of the three most important words he can hear.)

10. Offer to take a message. Never advise the person to call back. Doing so suggests her time is less valuable than your own.

11. Pretend you are an outsider and listen to the music or message being played while the person is on hold. Is the recording professional? Is it too loud?

12. Use courteous and comforting language, particularly if the caller is upset.

13. Don't make promises or speak for other people.

14. Avoid slang or jargon which the caller may not understand.

15. Speak in full sentences.

16. Remain calm if the person is calling to complain. It requires considerable maturity and professionalism to maintain your poise while the caller may be irately recounting the treatment received or the failure of the product. However, you must do all you can to ensure that you are representing yourself *and* your company well.

17. Make certain when you are screening calls that you do not create the impression that the caller is not important enough to be spoken to. If you say, "Mr. Jones is busy now," it suggests that he is too busy for you.

If you ask for the caller's name, it suggests that you will give it to the boss who is in her office. If you then come on the line and say the boss is <u>not</u> available, it appears that if your name had been a more important one, the boss would have spoken to you. It's better to say something like, "I'll check to see if she's available. May I ask who is calling?"

18. Do not permit a perceptible change in your voice once you learn the person's name. Be courteous to everyone!

19. Protect your fellow employees or superiors. You need not lie, but you need not choose words which may suggest improper or unprofessional behavior. Simply say, "Mr. Jones is not available at the moment." rather than "Mr. Jones is still out for lunch." (at three in the afternoon). Similarly, there is no need to say, "I haven't seen her for the last three hours" or "She hasn't come in yet" (at ten in the morning).

20. Learn as much as you can about your company and its people. Keep a list near the phone of answers to questions frequently asked. Such a list will save you time and create an impression of competence.

21. Write quickly, reducing the message to its bare bones.

22. Do not interrupt the caller.

23. Practice your speaking until you have achieved a well-modulated tone and volume.

24. Answer the phone with your full name.

25. Do not call executives at home unless the matter is a critical one.

26. When calling someone else, make your message concise and specific, particularly if you are delivering vital information (or information which the other person may perceive as vital).

27. Do not address someone whom you have never met by her first name.

Communicate with Quality

28. Do not have a subordinate place a phone call for you to a senior executive. To keep such a person waiting violates the rules of business protocol.

29. Do not take or make phone calls if you have someone sitting in your office.

30. Do not use the word "minute" or "second" when referring to the length of time the person will be on hold.

31. Do not give out home telephone numbers. Instead, offer to pass along the message to the person being called. Take the caller's name and number, but do not promise he or she will be called back.

32. Do not become too familiar with frequent callers. Always maintain a business-like demeanor.

What are other suggestions you can make for proper use of the telephone?

33. _____

34. _____

35. _____

36. _____

37. _____

38. _____

39. _____

40. _____

An Assessment Assignment

If you feel fairly confident about the telephone image you are projecting, here is an assignment to validate your impression of the impression you create. During the course of the coming week, ask five or ten different people (ideally those outside the company who do not know you well) to assess your telephone personality. Explain (at the end of the telephone conversation -- not the beginning) that you are part of a training program concerning telephone techniques and that you have been asked to obtain feedback concerning the image you project. Ask the caller to evaluate you honestly on a scale of 1 to 10, not only for that particular phone call but for your telephone personality on other occasions as well. Tally your scores and then average them. You may be surprised at the results.

Brainstorming Exercises:

Motivational Systems, a managment development firm, recently surveyed 200 corporate vice presidents and found they wasted at least a month every year on unnecessary or unproductive telephone calls. Their recommendations to the executives apply as well to other office professionals:

Decide what you will say before you place the call. Perhaps even take notes about the points you need to make or questions you need to ask.

Control the telephone conversation by not permitting it to ramble onto unrelated topics and by ending the conversation decisively.

Evaluate the importance of the call. If it does not have to be made, don't make it.

Now select an area that you feel could be enhanced in the workplace. It may be improved productivity via phone usage, or via meetings or reports or any of the numerous other requirements that constitute our jobs. Then join with at least two other colleagues to brainstorm ways to improve office efficiency.

Use the following page to brainstorm first your own ideas and then the group's ideas.

Communicate with Quality

Area to be analyzed for improvement: _____

My thoughts on this topic: _____

_____

_____

_____

_____

_____

_____

_____

Use the following space to make further notes as you work with other employees to ascertain ways to improve your work processes.

_____

_____

_____

_____

_____

_____

A widely accepted observation in the business world is that power does not flow to invisible people. Increasing your visibility will not only accelerate your climb up the corporate ladder, it will also produce impressive rewards: *you* will be rewarded with greater job satisfaction and the *company* will be rewarded with the excellence of your ideas.

In the space below, begin to prepare a document (perhaps for the company newsletter, perhaps for a proposal to your boss) that will encourage others to adopt the suggestions you and your colleagues made for improving some aspect of the work you do. Make your presentation clear, comprehensible, cohesive and--above all--convincing!

Customers, Culture, Co-operation

Write down quickly what you believe your organization's mission, or strategic goal, or main function to be:

_____

_____

_____

_____

_____

Next, explain how your particular job parallels or helps achieve the goal you described above:

_____

_____

_____

_____

_____

_____

_____

_____

American firms have moved from a product-driven to a market-driven to a technology-driven to, finally, a customer-driven mindset. And to fully implement that focus on total customer satisfaction, each employee must understand how he or she contributes to the firm's overall mission. Without customers, most employees would be unemployed, so it is to our advantage to win over customers and callers. Ideally, they will hang up saying "Wow!" after dealing with you on the phone.

TELEPHONE TIPS AND TECHNIQUES

Clearly, one important way of satisfying customers is listening to them carefully. Experts estimate that billions of dollars are lost each year because of listening failures within the corporate culture. It is harder to listen when you are on the phone, but there are some things you can do to ensure that you, as a representative of your firm, are as valuable an asset as the products or the technology or the inventory.

1. **Commit to listening.**
2. Recognize that every caller is important.
3. Realize that you may be creating the first impression of your corporation. Your front-line behavior may cause that customer to be won or lost.
4. Don't interrupt or try to cut the speaker off.
5. Find out what the caller really wants.
6. Listen "between the lines."
7. Employ verbal assurances.
8. Give feedback.
9. Verify numbers.
10. Summarize the call before hanging up.
11. Avoid saying "Have a nice day."
12. Make notes immediately after important calls.
13. Answer a ringing phone, even if it's not your own.
14. Whenever the phone rings, think to yourself, "That's my job calling!"

Try to implement these suggestions within twenty-four hours and continue to use them for a full two weeks. The research shows that immediate

Communicate with Quality

reinforcement of newly acquired skills improves the chance of those skills being retained!

Remember, anyone who uses the phone to deal with others is an ambassador whose knowledge of telephone protocol can either encumber or enhance the organization's efforts towards excellence.

Finally, these suggestions will help when you have to apologize for an error or delay which has caused the caller some inconvenience. (You can use these same suggestions for letters of apology that you may have to write.)

1. If some of the blame is yours, admit it.

2. State specifically how the problem came about.

3. Tell the caller tactfully what you can and can't do about the situation. If you have to say "no," do so with velvet gloves -- not a sledgehammer.

4. Express sincere regret but do not gush apologies. Don't say it will never happen again. Simply reassure the caller that you will do all you can to reduce the chances for future errors or delays.

5. End the conversation on a positive note. Do not bring the problem up all over again. Imply that good relations can be continued in future transactions. Remember that your mission is to persuade others to maintain their patronage of your firm.

Additional Affect-Ameliorating Activities

Here are oxymorons or self-contradicting expressions, from the Greek "oxy" meaning "wise" and "moron" meaning "fool." Can you think of others?

cruel kindness
make haste slowly
night light
light heavyweight
pretty ugly
inside out
dotted line
bridegroom
dry martini
bittersweet
majority of one
inconclusive conclusion
nonconforming conformist
militant pacifist
stupid know-it-all
cold sweat
impossible hope
living dead
dull shine
formless shape
civil war
backside
slow speed
scheduled delay
medium rare
black light
sounds of silence
hard cushion
negative assurance
drag race
second best
peacekeeper missile
uneasy calm
midnight sun
same difference

Communicate with Quality

Portmanteaux

Portmanteaux are words which are created by taking the first letter(s) of one word and the last few letters of another word to create a whole new word related to the original two. (Do not confuse portmanteaux with the addition of affixes to root words.) Here are some common portmanteaux. Can you find (or create) others?

smog (smoke + fog)
avionics (aviation + electronics)
brunch (breakfast + lunch)
broast (broil + roast)
camcorder (camera + recorder)
skorts (skirt + shorts)
motel (motor + hotel)
transponder (transmitter + responder)
transceiver (transmitter + receiver)
gasohol (gasoline + alcohol)
Palmcaster (Palmdale + Lancaster)
tangelo (tangerine + pomelo)
telecast (television + broadcast)
simulcast (simultaneous + broadcast)
Eurasian (European + Asian)
dramedy (drama + comedy)
ammeter (ampere + meter)
craze (crack + glaze)
spork (spoon + fork)
limon (lime + lemon)
futurama (future + panorama)
smice (smoke + ice)
beefalo (beef + buffalo)
snofari (snow + safari)
electrolier (electric + chandelier)
travelogue (travel + monologue)
caplet (capsule + tablet)
craisin (cranberry + raisin)
advertorial (advertisement + editorial)
evention (event + invention)
stagflation (stagnant + inflation)
reminessence (reminisce + essence)
fontasy (font + fantasy)

Communicate with Quality

Punctuation Prowess

Can you bring sense to the following through the use of punctuation marks?

WHERE JOHN HAD HAD HAD MARY HAD HAD HAD HAD HAD HAD HAD HAD THE TEACHERS APPROVAL

WOMAN WITHOUT HER MAN IS A BEAST

THAT THAT IS IS THAT THAT IS NOT IS NOT IS NOT THAT IT IT IS

HE SAID THAT THAT THAT THAT THAT THAT WRITER USED WAS UNNECESSARY

MRS. JONES' KIDNEY WAS IMPLANTED IN DR. BELL'S OPINION

The most valuable of all talents is that of never using two words when one will do.
—Thomas Jefferson

ANSWER KEY

Page 17

1. Twinkle, twinkle, little star. 2. Beginner's luck. 3. You can't teach an old dog new tricks. 4. Beauty is only skin deep. 5. The pen is mightier than the sword. 6. Look before you leap. 7. Birds of a feather flock together. 8. Don't cry over spilt milk. 9. Cleanliness is next to godliness. 10. Spare the rod and spoil the child.

Page 25 (Suggested Answers)

1. You will be reimbursed for tuition if you attend an accredited college. 2. Unfortunately, because of budget constraints, we cannot honor our secretaries these year as we would like to. However, each of them should be aware of our company's appreciation of their hard work and commitment. 3. In the future, please ensure that your assistant is fully aware of your schedule. 4. I wish you the best of luck on your new job. 5. I would appreciate your spending time with me so I can learn more about this subject. 6. We need not worry about dirty windows at this time. 7. Thank you for finding time to share your knowledge with me. 8. Thank you for your suggestion. We'll take it into consideration. 9. I believe we must implement this plan. 10. There will be a two-week delay in the shipment of your order. We regret any inconvenience it may cause you.

Page 32 (Note: Regard the first column as "A" and the second as "B."

1. A, 2. A, 3. B, 4. B, 5. A, 6. A, 7. B, 8. B, 9. A, 10. A, 11. B, 12. B, 13. A, 14. A, 15. B, 16. B, 17. A, 18. A, 19. B, 20. B, 21. A, 22. A, 23. B, 24. B, 25. A, 26. A, 27. B, 28. B, 29. A, 30. A, 31. B, 32. B, 33. A, 34. A, 35. B, 36. B, 37. A, 38. A, 39. B, 40. B, 41. A, 42. A, 43. B, 44. B, 45. A, 46. A, 47. B, 48. B, 49. A, 50. A.

Page 44

1. "0" 2. "Are you," she demanded, "the one in charge?" 3. George Bush, President of the United States, addressed the Business Roundtable yesterday. 4. The trainers' network, which has an international membership, provides many opportunities for self-growth. 5. While the year-end report was being prepared, the meeting was in progress. 6. She is definitely a "tweener." 7. period needed at end of sentence 8. Do you know any "dinks"? 9. "Fire!" she shouted. 10. I need, Mr. Jones, a new desk, a new typewriter (comma optional here) and a new desk chair. 11. June is--without a doubt--the most accurate typist in the department. (Commas are also acceptable in lieu of the dash.) 12. Therefore, I think we should consider a Southern state again next year; the planning committee concurs with my opinion. 13. The organization of the firm is quite simple: everyone reports to Mr. Jones. (The semicolon is also acceptable in lieu of the colon.) 14. Mr. Henry will use the famous "I have a dream..." line in his remarks tonight. 15. The names of the committee members are Lynette Day, EEO Officer; Susan Black, Vice President in Charge of International Trade; and Anthony Trollop, Public Relations Officer. 16. The fixed-price proposal (see Appendix II) incorporates the manufacturing changes required to produce the component. 17. Mr. Fujitani--despite what you may think--is actually the most committed member of the team. (Commas may also be used in lieu of dashes.) 18. His article, "The Impact of Interim Funding," will appear in the *Subcontractors Quarterly*. (Note: with book and magazine titles, you can either underline or use italics.) 19. She asks everyone, "Have you read Browning's poem, 'How Do I Love Thee?' " 20. The women's team has a better record than does the men's team. 21. He once wrote a letter to the Prince of Whales [sic]. 22. She has visited the site of Matthew Arnold's poem, "Dover Beach." 23. The bar graph (see page 14) depicts the escalation in our operating costs over the past twelve months. 24. The entire department--all 16 of us--is planning to take some vacation time during the month of June. (Note: commas or parentheses would also be acceptable, but the best mark here is the dash.) 25. Optometrists are the "apples of my eye."

Page 48

1. sister 2. "O" 3. University 4. "Don't 5. "O" 6. history 7. Uncle 8. "To whom it may concern." 9. the 10. Chinese 11. french fries 12. summer 13. "O" 14. he 15. "O" 16. what 17. "O" 18. "O" 19. synagogue 20. "O" 21. Bible 22. "O" 23. accounting 24. Fourth 25. truly

Page 50

1. Far East 2. Susan's/ yours. 3. Tompkins' (or Tompkin's)/ San Francisco,/twenty-four 4. "I'm/ Nevada,/ El Paso 5. said, "/ work." 6. Correct as written. (Note: the sentence could also be written, Hal boasted, "Our quality circle can do any job given to us." Also, in many companies, the words Quality Circle are capitalized.) 7. summer (Note: the comma after summer is optional.)/ after-hours 8. son-in-law's (Note: if there were two or more sons-in-law who went into business together, the word would be written as sons-in-law's.) 9. Ruskuff, Jr.,

10. ladies' Option: Ladies' (Note: think about the opposite of the ladies' room: it is the men's room. Both words should be written with an apostrophe. Option: third floor) 11. War/ Peace 12. Correct (Note: the actual title of an annual report would most likely have the year and the company's name in it.) 13. *Defense News* (Option: underline the title in lieu of italics.) 14. say, "Yes, Mr. Johnson. I'll be right there." 15. House Armed Services Committee

Page 52

1. me instead of I 2. me instead of I 3. correct 4. him instead of he 5. they instead of them 6. he instead of him 7. us instead of we 8. they instead of them 9. you and me instead of you and I 10. her instead of she 11. placing instead of the placement of 12. to postpone it instead of postponing it (Note: this sentence could also be written as Finishing a task is better than postponing it.) 13. distribute instead of the distribution of 14. simple to operate (Note: this sentence could also be written with nouns: economy, durability, and simplicity of operation.) 15. her desire instead of wanting 16. punctual or prompt instead of he is always on time. 17. bottlewashing to innkeeping is parallel; so is bottlewasher to innkeeper 18. women-owned businesses instead of women who own their own businesses 19. conditions instead of determining all the conditions. 20. to suggest instead of the suggestion of

Page 55

1. the second sentence 2. the second sentence 3. the second sentence 4. the second sentence 5. the second sentence 6. the second sentence 7. the second sentence 8. the second sentence 9. the first sentence 10. the first sentence 11. the first sentence 12. the second sentence 13. the second sentence 14. the second sentence 15. the second sentence

Page 57 (Note: there is more than one possible answer to each question. The answers must be expressed as the same part of speech as the original.)

1. sad, spurn 2. savant (smart is not acceptable since it is not a noun.), spouting 3. sell. single 4. specific, stubby 5. sanity, strangle 6. soothing, scattered 7. scarce, seek 8. scowl, shun 9. scrawl, sin 10. saintly, selfishness

Page 60

The letter "f" appears 35 times in this passage. (Don't overlook the word "of.")

Page 63, Exercise #3
1. looks instead of look, welcomes instead of welcome. (Note: the subject of the sentence is Each.) 2. To maximize our efforts, we will reserve the conference room for the entire day. 3. is instead of being 4. implementing instead of the implementation of 5. consensus instead of concensus of opinion/ no colon after be. (Option: seems to be the following:)

Page 65, Exercise #5

Make certain the title is underlined as it is in the original.

Page 66, Exercise #6 (Suggested Answers)

a. If you reject the proposal, please explain why so we can give the proposer a clear reason.
b. Please discuss the proposal with the person who submitted if after you have evaluated it. Let him or her know that we have interest in their ideas and in the success of the program itself.
c. We have established April 30, 1994, as a suspense date for adoption, rejection, or submission to a higher authority. If you cannot meet the date, notify this office.
d. Furnish the individuals listed below with an information copy of each transmittal document. Such action will keep the proposer aware of the status of his or her proposal.
e. Controversy has erupted between environmentalists and some government officials due to the operation of the parks. Some of the complex problems apparently resulted from a lack of foresight.
f. Authorities have identified 4,345 threats to park resources in a 1988 Congressional report titled "State of the Parks." Numerous causes, but also many possible cures, appear in that report.

Page 72, Exercise #10

1. accept 2. effect 3. hers 4. past 5. effect 6. except 7. affected 8. affect 9. illusionist 10. allusions 11. capital 12. capital 13. choose 14. chose (Note: it is possible to say choose if you were emphasizing the word You as you spoke this sentence.) 15. complements 16. compliment 17. complimentary 18. emigrant 19. eminent 20. imminent 21. principle 22. already 23. altogether 24. beside 25. their

Page 74, Exercise #11

1) My job is a highly rewarding one. I am continually challenged and find I can affect the lives of others in some small way. My boss accommodates my requests whenever he can. It's rewarding for me to be able to show other employees how their cooperative efforts can make a distinct difference (Note: the hyphenation was incorrect in the original.) in the company's overall effort. I've been here twenty-five years.

2) The specifics concerning the position are as follows:

Experience	Salary Increment	Notification Date
1-3 years' experience	$4,000	Monday, May 6
4-6 years' experience	$6,000	Monday, May 13
7-9 years' experience	$8,000	Monday, May 20

Page 74, Exercise #12

" 'Twas the night before Christmas and all through the house, not a creature was stirring...."

Page 80

1. hotel   2. debate   3. apt   4. fiction   5. rain   6. superior   7. tomb   8. round   9. part   10. face

Page 99

Where John had had "had," Mary had had "had had." "Had had" had had the teacher's approval.
Woman! Without her, man is a beast. (A different perspective on this sentence might yield,
    Woman--without her man--is a beast.)
That that is, is that that is not, is not. Is not that it? It is.
He said that that "that" that that that-writer used was unnecessary.
Mrs. Jones' kidney was implanted, in Dr. Bell's opinion. (Option: Begin the sentence with the last phrase.)